A Choice of
Sir Walter Ralegh's Verse

D0898918

by Robert Nye

BEE HUNTER: ADVENTURES OF BEOWULF

MARCH HAS HORSE'S EARS

TALIESIN

A CHOICE OF
Sir Walter Ralegh's Verse

selected
with an introduction by
ROBERT NYE

FABER AND FABER
3 Queen Square
London

First published in 1972
by Faber and Faber Limited
3 Queen Square London WC1
Printed in Great Britain by
Latimer Trend & Co Ltd Plymouth

ISBN 0 571 08753 1
(Faber Paper Covered Edition)

ISBN 0 571 08253 x
(Hard Bound Edition)

Contents

6

Editor's Note

The text of the poems in this selection is drawn from
Agnes M. C. Latham's *The Poems of Sir Walter Ralegh*
(1929; revised and supplemented, 1951). The original
spelling and punctuation have been preserved, but the
typography has been modernized. Miss Latham's is the
standard text, superseding Sir Egerton Brydges's *The
Poems of Sir Walter Raleigh* (1813) and Archdeacon Han-
nah's *The Poems of Sir Walter Raleigh collected and authenti-
cated with those of Sir Henry Wotton and other courtly poets
from 1540 to 1650* (1870). I am indebted to Miss Latham
and to Messrs. Routledge and Kegal Paul for permission
to reprint.

In two instances in this book a reading of Hannah's
has been preferred to one of Miss Latham's. These occur
in the ninth line of *Like to a Hermite poore* ('grief' for
'graie') and in line 473 of *The Ocean to Scinthia* ('rind' for
'vinde'). The poems *Feede still thy self, thou fondling with
beliefe, My first borne love unhappily conceived, A Secret murder
hath bene done of late* and *Sought by the world* are classified
under the heading 'conjectural' in Miss Latham's edition.
They are taken from the anthology *The Phoenix Nest*
(1593).

for
my wife
Aileen Campbell Nye

'true Love is a durable fyre'

Introduction

Sir Walter Ralegh excelled at other things besides the writing of poems, and it is for the other things that he is best known. 'Wholly gentleman, wholly soldier,' was his own description of himself at his trial in 1603. Disliked by many of his contemporaries for his pursuit of power and for what they took to be his arrogance when he had attained it, he was not commonly ambitious on behalf of his poetry and had no interest in its public dissemination. He seems to have belonged to a brilliant company of court wits, amateur poets, who permitted their work to circulate amongst themselves and their friends in manuscript but treated the literary market-place with disdain. George Puttenham describes them in his *Art of English Poesie* (1589):

> And in Her Majesty's time that now is, are sprung up another crew of courtly makers, noblemen and gentlemen of Her Majesty's own servants, who have written excellently well, as it would appear if their doings could be found out and made public with the rest, of which number is first that noble gentleman, Edward, Earl of Oxford, Thomas, Lord of Buckhurst (when he was young), Henry Lord Paget, Sir Philip Sidney, Sir Walter Ralegh, Master Edward Dyer, Master Fulke Greville, Gascoigne, Breton, Turberville and a great many other learned gentlemen, whose names I do not omit for envy, but to avoid tediousness, and who have deserved no little commendation.

Ralegh, as it happened, had better reason than most for not publishing. Many of his poems were addressed to the Queen, and not as some vague Gloriana, a national muse, but as a real woman, a royal mistress.

He was born at Hayes Barton, near Budleigh Salterton, in Devonshire, in 1552 or 1554, the younger son of a country gentleman of 'reduced estate'. John Aubrey reports that Ralegh 'spake broad Devonshire' all his life, and this accent can be made out in the spellings of words in *The Ocean to Scinthia*, discovered among the Cecil Papers in Hatfield House in the 1860's, one of his few holograph manuscripts to have survived. As a young man Ralegh spent a little time at Oriel College, Oxford, before going off to join English volunteers fighting on the side of the Huguenots in the French Wars of Religion. He was about five years in France. When he came back he took up residence for a while at the Inns of Court, in London, and from this period dates the first poem of his that we have—the rather sententious piece recommending George Gascoigne's *The Steele Glas* (1576). Gascoigne, whose merits were recently rediscovered with enthusiasm by the American critic Yvor Winters, is a poet of great plainness and bluntness. Ralegh's approval of him is revealing. It suggests that at an early age he already favoured a style of extreme simplicity.

A contemporary, Lord Grey of Wilton, whom he had helped in suppressing the Desmond Rebellion in Ireland, wrote of 'Captain Rawley' at this time: 'For mine own part, I must be plain: I neither like his carriage nor his company.' Ralegh was not much concerned with pleasing the Greys of the world. He was interested in the highest favours only. By 1580—by what means is not certainly known—he had won them. Elizabeth smiled on him. For twelve years thereafter he was one of the most powerful men in the kingdom, knighted in 1584, appointed Captain of the Guard in 1587, in which role he was held personally responsible for the Queen's safety. Ralegh's high career as royal favourite has been sufficiently chronicled by his biographers. His magnificence offended many. He is supposed to have spent a king's ransom on a jewel for his shoe. There is also talk of a white suit with jewels 'to the value of three-score thousand pounds'. These legends may be absurd, but they tell us something of the impression he made on paler envious souls. 'The best hated man in the world,' wrote Sir Anthony Bagot in 1587. The fall came five years later, in 1592, when his secret marriage to one of the royal maids of honour, Elizabeth Throckmorton, brought down the Queen's fury on his head. After a spell of imprisonment in the Tower, he was freed to live on his estate at Sherborne, in Dorset, and eventually to pursue fresh fortunes against Spain at sea and to lead a voyage of exploration to Guiana, but it was another five years before Elizabeth would allow him back to court. If her displeasure seems out of proportion to his offence, we have to remember that the Queen's maids of honour were sometimes looked upon as Vestal Virgins. Ralegh had insulted Elizabeth doubly by carrying one of them off while he was supposed to be devoted to the Queen alone. It has been presumed that he wrote *The Ocean to Scinthia* in the Tower at the time of his disgrace.

In 1603 Elizabeth died, and James VI of Scotland became James I of England. Within a matter of months Ralegh found that he had many enemies who had only been waiting for the removal of the Queen's protecting hand to bring about his overthrow. He was arrested and brought to trial on a charge of having conspired to dethrone James and lay England under Spanish dominion. The evidence of his guilt is unconvincing, and the possibility of his interest in such a plot seems slight, but he was convicted and condemned to death. The letters Ralegh wrote to comfort his wife at this point tell us much of the essence of the man. They speak with the same grave decent voice that is to be heard in the poetry:

You shall receave, deare wief, my last words in these my last lynes. My love I send you, that you may keepe it when I am dead; and my councell, that you may remember it when I am noe more. I would not, with my last Will, present you with sorrowes, deare Besse. Lett them goe to the grave with me, and be buried in the dust. And, seeing it is not the will of God that ever I shall see you in this lief, beare my destruction gentlie and with a hart like yourself.

First, I send you all the thanks my hart cann conceive, or my penn expresse, for your many troubles and cares taken for me, which—though they have not taken effect as you wished—yet my debt is to you never the lesse; but pay it I never shall in this world.

Secondlie, I beseich you, for the love you bare me living, that you doe not hide yourself many dayes, but by your travell seeke to helpe your miserable fortunes, and the right of your poore childe. Your mourning cannot avayle me that am but dust. . . .

Remember your poore childe for his father's sake, that comforted you and loved you in his happiest tymes. . . . And know itt (deare wief) that your sonne is the childe of a true man, and who, in his own respect, despiseth Death, and all his misshapen and ouglie formes.

I cannot wright much. God knowes howe hardlie I stole this tyme, when all sleep; and it is tyme to separate my thoughts from the world. Begg my dead body, which living was denyed you. . . . I can wright noe more. Tyme and Death call me awaye. . . . Your's that was; but nowe not my owne, W. Ralegh.

For reasons that have never been made clear, James decided on a reprieve at the last minute. Ralegh remained in the Tower for the next thirteen years. He occupied himself by writing a *History of the World*, though in constant ill health. In 1616, at the age of sixty-two, he was released but not pardoned, having succeeded in interesting James in the idea of an expedition to open a gold mine in Guiana. The conditions the King placed upon this venture doomed it from the start, for Ralegh was under strict orders to do nothing that would give offence to Spain, while being well aware that the Spanish considered Guiana their territory. In the event, the mine was not found, Ralegh's son was killed in a skirmish at a Spanish outpost, and Ralegh returned to England to be executed on the charge still obtaining from 1603. He died, as he had lived, bravely and with great style. 'He seemed as free from all manner of apprehension,' wrote an observer, Thomas Larkin, 'as if he had been come hither rather to be a spectator than a sufferer.' He forgave the executioner and would not be blindfolded. Asked if he did not wish to put his head down upon the block facing east, in hope of Christ's resurrection, he answered that it was no great matter which way the head lay, 'so the heart be right'.

Ralegh's remark about the heart being right is his answer to the age that made him and broke him. The accent of that answer—proud, implacable, serious—rings through his poetry. So does the urgency of its occasion, for Ralegh wrote poems only when he had to. Because of this admirable habit he has been patronized by some literary commentators as an 'amateur', but this judgement could not be pressed too far in face of the actual poems. If clarity and craftsmanship count for anything then he is expert. His voice is his own, and unmistakable—*lofty, insolent, and passionate*, as a contemporary, George Puttenham, describes it. We have, of course, a modern critical cliché regarding the desirability of a poet finding his own 'voice', generally meaning little more than that the poet in question has managed not to sound too much like other poets. This concept of 'voice' becomes pertinent and precise, though, when applied to a poet as plain-spoken as Ralegh, for it is indeed the levelness of his tone, the deliberation of his thought, and the quality and consistency of his feeling—in a word, the *integrity* of his utterance—which gives his verse its particular character. His least line bears the imprint of a strong and independent mind with something to say and complete command of the ways of saying, but if any whole poem be considered then as likely as not it will be found that the poet is subscribing to a traditional view of things and subduing his verbal excitement to a fairly well-worn range of imagery in doing so. It is the difference between the personal tone and the impersonal sense which is impressive in lines like these:

> *Even such is tyme which takes in trust*
> *Our yowth, our Joyes, and all we have,*
> *And payes us butt with age and dust:*
> *Who in the darke and silent grave*
> *When we have wandred all our wayes*
> *Shutts up the storye of our dayes.*
> *And from which earth and grave and dust*
> *The Lord shall rayse me up I trust.*

For all the tricky problems of textual authenticity—for discussion of which the interested reader is referred to Agnes Latham's very full coverage of the matter in the notes to her complete edition—I think that Ralegh's voice is easy to hear and, once heard, to recognize. *The Nimphs reply to the Sheepheard*, for example, is very much in the same spirit as his 'so the heart be right' remark to Dean Tounson on the scaffold. There is a difference of emphasis, of course—the poem verges on the cynical, while the riposte is deadly serious—but both evince a witty insistence upon certain fundamental virtues which one might term poetic if one did not still hope that they might be more comprehensively 'human'—the importance of unsentimental clarity, the kind of self-possession that goes with an intense commitment to language as a means of putting thought and feeling to the test, a complementary refusal to be seduced by any sort of 'glamour'. Ralegh's 'nimph' is more self-aware than Marlowe's 'sheepheard' bargained for. The voice heard in this acid brush-off seems to me that of a poet ready to place himself, without affectation, above comfortable judgement and beyond ordinary opinion. The same voice speaks in *The Lie*, haughty and imperative, only here—stung to insult by contempt—Ralegh leaves off bantering and writes as though fighting a duel with his age:

> *Say to the Court it glowes,*
> *   and shines like rotten wood,*
> *Say to the Church it showes*
> *   what's good, and doth no good.*
> *If Church and Court reply,*
> *   then give them both the lie.*

In gentler vein, but still insisting on its own seriousness, it can also be heard at the conclusion of *As you came from the holy land*, one of Ralegh's most moving and memorable poems, where he takes a popular ballad (bits of which were remembered by Ophelia in her delirium) and makes it strangely his own before adding a characteristic contrast of the confusions of false love and its lucid opposite:

> *Of women kynde suche indeed is the love*
> *   Or the word Love abused*
> *Under which many chyldysh desyres*
> *   And conceytes are excusde.*
>
> *Butt true Love is a durable fyre*
> *   In the mynde ever burnynge;*
> *Never sycke, never ould, never dead,*
> *   From itt selfe never turnynge.*

The intelligence and feeling behind that *but* are absolutely to the point. Ralegh is the poet of but. No other Elizabethan uses the conjunction so tellingly or makes so much hinge on it in attacking the false and declaring his allegiance to the true.

There is an aptness in the gossip that ascribes several of Ralegh's pieces to 'the night before he died', 'supposed to be written by one at the point of death', and so on. His best work has the truthful urgency of someone facing things finally, possessed by a need to say what he has to say as plainly and briefly as possible. If his last words on the block sound like a line of his poetry so do the lines of his poetry sound very often like Last Words: the summary of a lifetime's experience. The exotic and exuberant imagery of *The passionate mans Pilgrimage* might be taken to give the lie to this observation. Lines like

> *Then the holy paths weele travell*
> *Strewde with Rubies thicke as gravell,*
> *Seelings of Diamonds, Saphire floores,*
> *High walles of Corall and Pearle Bowres*

are so rich that it is hard to conceive of them being written by the man who otherwise compressed his faith and despair to the gritty aphorism: *Onely we dye in earnest, that's no Jest*. But Ralegh was capable of writing with uncharacteristic abandon on occasion. Because he knew his craft so thoroughly and sincerely he could—under the most extreme mental or emotional pressure—allow himself to forget himself and his craft and write whatever came from deeper areas of knowing, and from the depths of unknowing. At such times he was a great poet. The *Pilgrimage* marks such a time; so does *The Ocean to Scinthia*.

This last-mentioned poem seems to me Ralegh's finest achievement. There is nothing much like it in English poetry until you come to T. S. Eliot's *The Waste Land*, where a comparable despair and sense of deprivation even throws up similar images in its course. *The Ocean to Scinthia* resembles *The Waste Land* also in that it is fragmented, fragmentary—and we touch here on a point that I mention with diffidence, for Agnes Latham and others have expressed themselves of the opinion that this poem is not an achievement, however interesting, however packed with brilliant lines and passages, because it fails when judged by certain Elizabethan standards of decorum and coherence. The impassioned character of the verse, its lack of polish and smoothness, as well as the abruptness with which it switches from mood to mood, theme to theme, displaying what Miss Latham very well defines as 'a perpetual flux and reflux of contrary feeling', all this tends to support the argument that the poem is more obsessive than understandable, but only if the whole is read as an attempt to be what I think it is not trying to be—a coherent *narrative*. Read as that, *The Waste Land* would also be found wanting. The comparison is not so far-fetched either, for it is my contention that Ralegh's poem, as surely as Eliot's, is a *deliberate fragment*, and that its fractured sense and burning obscurity, consuming its own images as a bonfire its bones, are all part of the intention. The way it is written, that is to say, is part of its 'meaning'. It is a dark way, but then it is a dark poem. Besides, it is also a brilliant poem, a brilliant way.

I have for this selection chosen what I take to be Ralegh's essential poems. Not many have had to be left out, for time and mischance have criticized Ralegh harshly. Perhaps, though, there was never a great body of work. I have even wondered—despite Edmund Spenser—whether the other books of *The Ocean to Scinthia* were ever written. 'He was sometimes a poet,' writes Aubrey, 'not often.' But that is true of many who wrote ten times as much. What has survived of Ralegh is sufficient.

ROBERT NYE

Edinburgh
December 1969

Walter Rawely of the middle Temple, in commendation of the Steele Glasse

Swete were the sauce would please ech kind of tast;
The life likewise were pure that never swerved;
For spyteful tongs in cankred stomackes plaste,
Deeme worst of things which best (percase) deserved:
But what for that? this medcine may suffyse,
To scorne the rest, and seke to please the wise.

Though sundry mindes in sundry sorte do deeme,
Yet worthiest wights yelde prayse for every payne;
But envious braynes do nought (or light) esteme,
Such stately steppes as they cannot attaine.
For whoso reapes renowne above the rest,
With heapes of hate shal surely be opprest.

Wherefore to write my censure of this booke;
This Glasse of Steele unpartially doth shewe,
Abuses all, to such as in it looke,
From prince to poore, from high estate to lowe,
As for the verse, who list like trade to trye,
I feare me much, shal hardly reache so high.

A Poem put into my Lady Laiton's pocket by Sir W. Rawleigh

Lady farwell whom I in Sylence serve
 Wold god thou knewste the depth of my desire,
Then might I hope, thoughe nought I can deserve,
 Som drop of grace wold quench my scorchyng fyre.
But as to Love unknowne I have decreed,
So spare to speake doth often spare to speed.

Yett better twere that I in woe should waste
 Then sue for Grace and Pyty in Despighte,
And though I see in thee such pleasure plaste
 That feedes my Joy and breedes my cheef delyghte,
Wythall I see a chast Consentt Dysdayne
Theyr Suytes, whych seke to wyn thy wyll ageane.

Then farewell Hope and Hellpe to each mans Harme
 The wynde of woe hath torne my Tree of Truste,
Care Quenchde the Coales, whych did my Fancy warme,
 And all my Hellp Lyes buryed in the Duste.
But yett amonges those Cares, which Crosse my Rest,
Thys Comfort Growes, I thynke I Love thee Beste.

An Epitaph upon the right Honorable sir Philip Sidney knight: Lord governor of Flushing (died 1586)

To praise thy life, or waile thy woorthie death,
And want thy wit, thy wit high, pure, divine,
Is far beyond the powre of mortall line,
Nor any one hath worth that draweth breath.

Yet rich in zeale, though poore in learnings lore,
And friendly care obscurde in secret brest,
And love that envie in thy life supprest,
Thy deere life done, and death hath doubled more.

And I, that in thy time and living state,
Did onely praise thy vertues in my thought,
As one that seeld the rising sunne hath sought,
With words and teares now waile thy timelesse fate.

Drawne was thy race, aright from princely line,
Nor lesse than such, (by gifts that nature gave,
The common mother that all creatures have,)
Doth vertue shew, and princely linage shine.

A king gave thee thy name, a kingly minde,
That God thee gave, who found it now too deere
For this base world, and hath resumde it neere,
To sit in skies, and sort with powres divine.

Kent thy birth daies, and Oxford held thy youth,
The heavens made haste, and staide nor yeeres, nor time,
The fruits of age grew ripe in thy first prime,
Thy will, thy words; thy words, the seales of truth.

Great gifts and wisedome rare imploide thee thence,
To treat from kings, with those more great than kings,
Such hope men had to lay the highest things,
On thy wise youth, to be transported hence.

Whence to sharpe wars sweete honor did thee call,
Thy countries love, religion, and thy friends:
Of woorthy men, the marks, the lives and ends,
And her defence, for whom we labor all.

There didst thou vanquish shame and tedious age,
Griefe, sorow, sicknes, and base fortunes might:
Thy rising day, saw never wofull night,
But past with praise, from off this worldly stage.

Backe to the campe, by thee that day was brought,
First thine owne death, and after thy long fame;
Teares to the soldiers, the proud Castilians shame;
Vertue exprest, and honor truly taught.

What hath he lost, that such great grace hath woon,
Yoong yeeres, for endles yeeres, and hope unsure,
Of fortunes gifts, for wealth that still shall dure,
Oh happie race with so great praises run.

England doth hold thy lims that bred the same,
Flaunders thy valure where it last was tried,
The Campe thy sorrow where thy bodie died,
Thy friends, thy want; the world, thy vertues fame.

Nations thy wit, our mindes lay up thy love,
Letters thy learning, thy losse, yeeres long to come,
In worthy harts sorow hath made thy tombe,
Thy soule and spright enrich the heavens above.

Thy liberall hart imbalmd in gratefull teares.
Yoong sighes, sweete sighes, sage sighes, bewaile thy fall,
Envie hir sting, and spite hath left hir gall,
Malice hir selfe, a mourning garment weares.

That day their Haniball died, our Scipio fell,
Scipio, Cicero, and Petrarch of our time,
Whose vertues wounded by my woorthles rime,
Let Angels speake, and heavens thy praises tell.

A Farewell to false Love

Farewell false love, the oracle of lies,
A mortal foe and enimie to rest:
An envious boye, from whome all cares arise,
A bastard vile, a beast with rage possest:
A way of error, a temple ful of treason,
In all effects, contrarie unto reason.

A poysoned serpent covered all with flowers,
Mother of sighes, and murtherer of repose,
A sea of sorows from whence are drawen such showers,
As moysture lend to everie griefe that growes,
A schole of guile, a net of deepe deceit,
A guilded hooke, that holds a poysoned bayte.

A fortresse foyld, which reason did defend,
A Syren song, a feaver of the minde,
A maze whcrein affection finds no ende,
A ranging cloude that runnes before the winde,
A substance like the shadow of the Sunne,
A goale of griefe for which the wisest runne.

A quenchlesse fire, a nurse of trembling feare,
A path that leads to perill and mishap,
A true retreat of sorrow and dispayre,
An idle boy that sleepes in pleasures lap,
A deepe mistrust of that which certaine seemes,
A hope of that which reason doubtfull deemes.

Syth then thy traynes my yonger yeers betrayd
And for my fayth ingratitude I fynde.
And sythe repentaunce hathe my wrongs bewrayde
Whose course was ever contrarye to kynde.
False Love; Desyre; and Bewty frayll adewe
Dead is the roote whence all these fancyes grewe.

The Excuse

Calling to minde mine eie long went about,
T'entice my hart to seeke to leave my brest,
All in a rage I thought to pull it out,
By whose device I liv'd in such unrest,
    What could it say to purchase so my grace?
    Forsooth that it had seene my Mistres face.

Another time I likewise call to minde,
My hart was he that all my woe had wrought,
For he my brest the fort of Love resignde,
When of such warrs my fancie never thought,
    What could it say, when I would him have slaine?
    But he was yours, and had forgone me cleane.

At length when I perceiv'd both eie and hart,
Excusde themselves, as guiltles of mine ill,
I found my selfe was cause of all my smart,
And tolde my selfe, my selfe now slay I will:
    But when I found my selfe to you was true,
    I lov'd my selfe, bicause my selfe lov'd you.

Praisd be Dianas faire and harmles light

Praisd be Dianas faire and harmles light,
Praisd be the dewes, wherwith she moists the ground;
Praisd be hir beames, the glorie of the night,
Praisd be hir powre, by which all powres abound.

Praisd be hir Nimphs, with whom she decks the woods,
Praisd be hir knights, in whom true honor lives,

Praisd be that force, by which she moves the floods,
Let that Diana shine, which all these gives.

In heaven Queene she is among the spheares,
In ay she Mistres like makes all things pure,
Eternitie in hir oft chaunge she beares,
She beautie is, by hir the faire endure.

Time weares hir not, she doth his chariot guide,
Mortalitie belowe hir orbe is plaste,
By hir the vertue of the starrs downe slide,
In hir is vertues perfect image cast.

A knowledge pure it is hir worth to kno,
With Circes let them dwell that thinke not so.

Like to a Hermite poore

Like to a Hermite poore in place obscure,
I meane to spend my daies of endles doubt,
To waile such woes as time cannot recure,
Where none but Love shall ever finde me out.

My foode shall be of care and sorow made,
My drink nought else but teares falne from mine eies,
And for my light in such obscured shade,
The flames shall serve, which from my hart arise.

A gowne of grief, my bodie shall attire,
My staffe of broken hope whereon Ile staie,
Of late repentance linckt with long desire,
The couch is fram'de whereon my limbs Ile lay,

27

And at my gate dispaire shall linger still,
To let in death when Love and Fortune will.

Farewell to the Court

Like truthles dreames, so are my joyes expired,
And past returne, are all my dandled daies:
My love misled, and fancie quite retired,
Of all which past, the sorow onely staies.

My lost delights now cleane from sight of land,
Have left me all alone in unknowne waies:
My minde to woe, my life in fortunes hand,
Of all which past, the sorow onely staies.

As in a countrey strange without companion,
I onely waile the wrong of deaths delaies,
Whose sweete spring spent, whose sommer well nie don,
Of all which past, the sorow onely staies.

Whom care forewarnes, ere age and winter colde,
To haste me hence, to find my fortunes folde.

Feede still thy selfe, thou fondling
with beliefe

Feede still thy selfe, thou fondling with beliefe,
Go hunt thy hope, that never tooke effect,
Accuse the wrongs that oft hath wrought thy griefe,
And reckon sure where reason would suspect.

Dwell in the dreames of wish and vain desire,
Pursue the faith that flies and seekes to new,
Run after hopes that mocke thee with retire,
And looke for love where liking never grew.

Devise conceits to ease thy carefull hart,
Trust upon times and daies of grace behinde,
Presume the rights of promise and desart,
And measure love by thy beleeving minde.

Force thy affects that spite doth daily chace,
Winke at the wrongs with wilfull oversight,
See not the soyle and staine of thy disgrace,
Nor recke disdaine, to doate on thy delite.

And when thou seest the end of thy reward,
And these effects ensue of thine assault,
When rashnes rues, that reason should regard,
Yet still accuse thy fortune for the fault.

 And crie, O Love, O death, O vaine desire,
 When thou complainst the heate, and feeds the fire.

My first borne love unhappily conceived

My first borne love unhappily conceived,
Brought foorth in paine, and christened with a curse
Die in your Infancie, of life bereaved,
  By your cruell nurse.

Restlesse desire, from my Love that proceeded,
Leave to be, and seeke your heaven by dieng,
Since you, O you? your owne hope have exceeded,
  By too hie flieng.

29

And you my words, my harts faithfull expounders,
No more offer your Jewell, unesteemed,
Since those eyes my Loves life and lives confounders,
        Your woorth misdeemed.

Love leave to desire, words leave it to utter,
Swell on my thoughts, till you breake that contains you
My complaints in those deafe eares no more mutter,
        That so disdaines you.

And you careles of me, that without feeling,
With drie eies, behold my Tragedie smiling,
Decke your proude triumphes with your poore slaves
   yeelding
        To his owne spoyling.

But if that wrong, or holy truth dispised,
To just revenge, the heavens ever moved,
So let hir love, and so be still denied,
        Who she so loved.

A Secret murder hath bene done of late

A Secret murder hath bene done of late,
Unkindnes founde, to be the bloudie knife,
And shee that did the deede a dame of state,
Faire, gracious, wise, as any beareth life.

To quite hir selfe, this answere did she make,
Mistrust (quoth she) hath brought him to his end,
Which makes the man so much himselfe mistake,
To lay the guilt unto his guiltles frend.

Ladie not so, not feard I found my death,
For no desart thus murdered is my minde,
And yet before I yeeld my fainting breath,
I quite the killer, tho I blame the kinde.

You kill unkinde, I die, and yet am true,
For at your sight, my wound doth bleede anew.

Sought by the world

Sought by the world, and hath the world disdain'd
Is she, my hart, for whom thou doost endure,
Unto whose grace, sith Kings have not obtaind,
Sweete is thy choise, though losse of life be sowre:
   Yet to the man, whose youth such pains must prove,
   No better end, than that which comes by Love.

Steere then thy course unto the port of death,
Sith thy hard hap no betrer hap may finde,
Where when thou shalt unlade thy latest breath,
Envie hir selfe shall swim to save thy minde,
   Whose bodie sunke in search to gaine that shore,
   Where many a Prince had perished before.

And yet my hart it might have been foreseene,
Sith skilfull medcins mends each kinde of griefe,
Then in my breast full safely hadst thou beene,
But thou my hart wouldst never me beleeve,
   Who tolde thee true, when first thou didst aspire,
   Death was the end of every such desire.

A Vision upon this conceipt of the Faery Queene

Methought I saw the grave, where *Laura* lay,
Within that Temple, where the vestall flame
Was wont to burne, and passing by that way,
To see that buried dust of living fame,
Whose tumbe faire love, and fairer vertue kept,
All suddeinly I saw the Faery Queene:
At whose approch the soule of *Petrarke* wept,
And from thenceforth those graces were not seene.
For they this Queene attended, in whose steed
Oblivion laid him downe on *Lauras* herse:
Hereat the hardest stones were seene to bleed,
And grones of buried ghostes the hevens did perse.
    Where *Homers* spright did tremble all for griefe,
    And curst th'accesse of that celestiall theife.

The Advice

Many desire, but few or none deserve
To win the Fort of thy most constant will:
Therefore take heed, let fancy never swerve
But unto him that will defend thee still.
    For this be sure, the fort of fame once won,
    Farewell the rest, thy happy dayes are done.

Many desire, but few or none deserve
To pluck the flowers and let the leaves to fall;
Therefore take heed, let fancy never swerve,
But unto him that will take leaves and all.
    For this be sure, the flower once pluckt away,
    Farewell the rest, thy happy days decay.

Many desire, but few or none deserve
To cut the corn, not subject to the sickle.
Therefore take heed, let fancy never swerve,
But constant stand, for Mowers mindes are fickle.
   For this be sure, the crop being once obtain'd
   Farewell the rest, the soil will be disdain'd.

The Nimphs reply to the Sheepheard

If all the world and love were young,
And truth in every Sheepheards tongue,
These pretty pleasures might me move,
To live with thee, and be thy love.

Time drives the flocks from field to fold,
When Rivers rage, and Rocks grow cold,
And Philomell becommeth dombe,
The rest complaines of cares to come.

The flowers doe fade, and wanton fieldes,
To wayward winter reckoning yeeldes,
A honny tongue, a hart of gall,
Is fancies spring, but sorrowes fall.

Thy gownes, thy shooes, thy beds of Roses,
Thy cap, thy kirtle, and thy poesies,
Soone breake, soone wither, soone forgotten:
In follie ripe, in reason rotten.

Thy belt of straw and Ivie buddes,
Thy Corall claspes and Amber studdes,
All these in mee no meanes can move,
To come to thee, and be thy love.

But could youth last, and love still breede,
Had joyes no date, nor age no neede,
Then these delights my minde might move,
To live with thee, and be thy love.

A Poesie to prove affection is not love

Conceipt begotten by the eyes,
Is quickly borne, and quickly dies:
For while it seekes our harts to have,
Meane while there Reason makes his grave:
For many things the eyes approve,
Which yet the hart doth seldome love.

For as the seedes in spring time sowne,
Die in the ground ere they be growne,
Such is conceipt, whose rooting failes,
As childe that in the cradle quailes,
Or else within the Mothers wombe,
Hath his beginning, and his tombe.

Affection followes Fortunes wheeles;
And soone is shaken from her heeles;
For following beautie or estate,
Hir liking still is turn'd to hate.
For all affections have their change,
And fancie onely loves to range.

Desire himselfe runnes out of breath,
And getting, doth but gaine his death:
Desire, nor reason hath, nor rest,
And blinde doth sildome chuse the best,
Desire attain'd is not desire,
But as the sinders of the fire.

As shippes in ports desir'd are drownd,
As fruit once ripe, then falles to ground,
As flies that seeke for flames, are brought
To cinders by the flames they sought:
So fond Desire when it attaines,
The life expires, the woe remaines.

And yet some Poets faine would prove,
Affection to be perfit love,
And that Desire is of that kinde,
No lesse a passion of the minde.
As if wilde beasts and men did seeke,
To like, to love, to chuse alike.

Sir Walter Ralegh to the Queen

Our Passions are most like to Floods and streames;
The shallow Murmure; but the Deep are Dumb.
So when Affections yeeld Discourse, it seems
The bottom is but shallow whence they come.
  They that are Rich in Words must needs discover
  That they are Poore in that which makes a Lover.

Wrong not, deare Empresse of my Heart,
  The Meritt of true Passion,
With thinking that Hee feels no Smart,
  That sues for no Compassion:

Since, if my Plaints serve not to prove
  The Conquest of your Beauty,
It comes not from Defect of Love,
  But from Excesse of duety.

For knowing that I sue to serve
    A Saint of such Perfection,
As all desire, but none deserve,
    A place in her Affection:
I rather chuse to want Reliefe
    Then venture the Revealing;
When Glory recommends the Griefe,
    Despaire distrusts the Healing.

Thus those desires that aime too high,
    For any mortall Lover,
When Reason cannot make them dye,
    Discretion will them Cover.
Yet when discretion dothe bereave
    The Plaints that they should utter,
Then your discretion may perceive,
    That Silence is a Suitor.

Silence in Love bewraies more Woe,
    Then Words, though ne'r so Witty,
A Beggar that is dumb, yee know,
    Deserveth double Pitty.
Then misconceive not (dearest Heart)
    My true, though secret Passion,
Hee smarteth most that hides his smart,
    And sues for no Compassion.

A Poem of Sir Walter Rawleighs: Nature that washt her hands in milke

Nature that washt her hands in milke
    And had forgott to dry them,

In stead of earth tooke snow and silke
 At Loves request to trye them,
If she a mistresse could compose
To please Loves fancy out of those.

Her eyes he would should be of light,
 A Violett breath, and Lipps of Jelly,
Her haire not blacke, nor over bright,
 And of the softest downe her Belly,
As for her inside hee'ld have it
Only of wantonnesse and witt.

At Loves entreaty, such a one
 Nature made, but with her beauty
She hath framed a heart of stone,
 So as Love by ill destinie
Must dye for her whom nature gave him
Because her darling would not save him.

But Time which nature doth despise,
 And rudely gives her love the lye,
Makes hope a foole, and sorrow wise,
 His hands doth neither wash, nor dry,
But being made of steele and rust,
Turnes snow, and silke, and milke to dust.

The Light, the Belly, lipps and breath,
 He dimms, discolours, and destroyes,
With those he feedes, but fills not death,
 Which sometimes were the foode of Joyes;
Yea Time doth dull each lively witt,
And dryes all wantonnes with it.

Oh cruell Time which takes in trust
 Our youth, our Joyes and all we have,

And payes us but with age and dust,
   Who in the darke and silent grave
When we have wandred all our wayes
Shutts up the story of our dayes.

As you came from the holy land

As you came from the holy land
   Of Walsinghame
Mett you not with my true love
   By the way as you came?

How shall I know your trew love
   That have mett many one
As I went to the holy lande
   That have come, that have gone?

She is neyther whyte nor browne
   Butt as the heavens fayre
There is none hathe a forme so divine
   In the earth or the ayre.

Such an one did I meet, good Sir,
   Suche an Angelyke face,
Who lyke a queene, lyke a nymph, did appere
   By her gate, by her grace.

She hath lefte me here all alone,
   All allone as unknowne,
Who somtymes did me lead with her selfe,
   And me lovde as her owne.

Whats the cause that she leaves you alone
    And a new waye doth take;
Who loved you once as her owne
    And her joye did you make?

I have lovde her all my youth,
    Butt now ould, as you see,
Love lykes not the fallyng frute
    From the wythered tree.

Know that love is a careless chylld
    And forgets promyse paste,
He is blynd, he is deaff when he lyste
    And in faythe never faste.

His desyre is a dureless contente
    And a trustless joye
He is wonn with a world of despayre
    And is lost with a toye.

Of women kynde suche indeed is the love
    Or the word Love abused
Under which many chyldysh desyres
    And conceytes are excusde.

Butt true Love is a durable fyre
    In the mynde ever burnynge;
Never sycke, never ould, never dead,
    From itt selfe never turnynge.

If Synthia be a Queene, a princes, and supreame

If Synthia be a Queene, a princes, and supreame,
Keipe thes amonge the rest, or say it was a dreame;

39

For thos that like, expound, and those that louth, express,
Meanings accordinge as their minds, ar moved more or
    less;
For writinge what thow art, or shewinge what thow
    weare;
Adds to the one dysdayne, to th'other butt dyspaire;
    Thy minde of neather needs, in both seinge it exceeds.

My boddy in the walls captived

My boddy in the walls captived
Feels not the wounds of spightfull envy,
Butt my thralde mind, of liberty deprived,
Fast fettered in her auntient memory,
Douth nought beholde butt sorrowes diinge face;
Such prison earst was so delightfull
As it desirde no other dwellinge place,
Butt tymes effects, and destinies dispightfull
Have changed both my keeper and my fare,
Loves fire, and bewties light I then had store,
Butt now close keipt, as captives wounted are,
That food, that heat, that light I finde no more,
    Dyspaire bolts up my dores, and I alone
    Speake to dead walls, butt thos heare not my mone.

The 11th: and last booke of the Ocean to Scinthia

Sufficeth it to yow my joyes interred,
In simpell wordes that I my woes cumplayne,
Yow that then died when first my fancy erred,
Joyes under dust that never live agayne.

If to the livinge weare my muse adressed,
Or did my minde her own spirrit still inhold,
Weare not my livinge passion so repressed,
As to the dead, the dead did thes unfold,

Sume sweeter wordes, sume more becumming vers,
Should wittness my myshapp in hygher kynd,
But my loves wounds, my fancy in the hearse,
The Idea but restinge, of a wasted minde,

The blossumes fallen, the sapp gon from the tree,
The broken monuments of my great desires,
From thes so lost what may th'affections bee,
What heat in Cynders of extinguisht fiers?

Lost in the mudd of thos hygh flowinge streames
Which through more fayrer feilds ther courses bend,
Slayne with sealf thoughts, amasde in fearfull dreams,
Woes without date, discumforts without end,

From frutfull trees I gather withred leves
And glean the broken eares with misers hands,
Who sumetyme did injoy the waighty sheves
I seeke faire floures amidd the brinish sand.

All in the shade yeven in the faire soon dayes
Under thos healthless trees I sytt alone,
Wher joyfull byrdds singe neather lovely layes
Nor Phillomen recounts her direfull mone.

No feedinge flockes, no sheapherds cumpunye
That might renew my dollorus consayte,
While happy then, while love and fantasye
Confinde my thoughts onn that faire flock to waite;

No pleasinge streames fast to the ocean wendinge
The messengers sumetymes of my great woe,
But all onn yearth as from the colde stormes bendinge
Shrinck from my thoughts in hygh heavens and below.

Oh hopefull love my object, and invention,
Oh, trew desire the spurr of my consayte,
Oh, worthiest spirrit, my minds impulsion,
Oh, eyes transpersant, my affections bayte,

Oh, princely forme, my fancies adamande,
Devine consayte, my paynes acceptance,
Oh, all in onn, oh heaven on yearth transparant,
The seat of joyes, and loves abundance!

Out of that mass of mirakells, my Muse,
Gathered thos floures, to her pure sences pleasinge,
Out of her eyes (the store of joyes) did chuse
Equall delights, my sorrowes counterpoysinge.

Her regall lookes, my rigarus sythes suppressed,
Small dropes of joies, sweetned great worlds of woes,
One gladsume day a thowsand cares redressed.
Whom Love defends, what fortune overthrowes?

When shee did well, what did ther elce amiss?
When shee did ill what empires could have pleased?
No other poure effectinge wo, or bliss,
Shee gave, shee tooke, shee wounded, shee apeased.

The honor of her love, Love still devisinge,
Woundinge my mind with contrary consayte,
Transferde it sealf sumetyme to her aspiringe
Sumetyme the trumpett of her thoughts retrayt;

To seeke new worlds, for golde, for prayse, for glory,
To try desire, to try love severed farr,
When I was gonn shee sent her memory
More stronge then weare ten thousand shipps of warr,

To call mee back, to leve great honors thought,
To leve my frinds, my fortune, my attempte,
To leve the purpose I so longe had sought
And holde both cares, and cumforts in contempt.

Such heat in Ize, such fier in frost remaynde,
Such trust in doubt, such cumfort in dispaire,
Mich like the gentell Lamm, though lately waynde,
Playes with the dug though finds no cumfort ther.

But as a boddy violently slayne
Retayneath warmth although the spirrit be gonn,
And by a poure in nature moves agayne
Till it be layd below the fatall stone;

Or as the yearth yeven in cold winter dayes
Left for a tyme by her life gevinge soonn,
Douth by the poure remayninge of his rayes
Produce sume green, though not as it hath dunn;

Or as a wheele forst by the fallinge streame,
Although the course be turnde sume other way
Douth for a tyme go rounde uppon the beame
Till wantinge strenght to move, it stands at stay;

So my forsaken hart, my withered mind,
Widdow of all the joyes it once possest,
My hopes cleane out of sight, with forced wind
To kyngdomes strange, to lands farr off addrest.

Alone, forsaken, frindless onn the shore
With many wounds, with deaths cold pangs inebrased,
Writes in the dust as onn that could no more
Whom love, and tyme, and fortune had defaced,

Of things so great, so longe, so manefolde
With meanes so weake, the sowle yeven then departing
The weale, the wo, the passages of olde
And worlds of thoughts discribde by onn last sythinge:

As if when after Phebus is dessended
And leves a light mich like the past dayes dawninge,
And every toyle and labor wholy ended
Each livinge creature draweth to his restinge

Wee should beginn by such a partinge light
To write the story of all ages past
And end the same before th'aprochinge night.

Such is agayne the labor of my minde
Whose shroude by sorrow woven now to end
Hath seene that ever shininge soonn declynde
So many yeares that so could not dissende

But that the eyes of my minde helde her beames
In every part transferd by loves swift thought;
Farr off or nire, in wakinge or in dreames,
Imagination stronge their luster brought.

Such force her angellike aparance had
To master distance, tyme, or crueltye,
Such art to greve, and after to make gladd,
Such feare in love, such love in majestye.

My weery lymes, her memory imbalmed,
My darkest wayes her eyes make cleare as day.
What stormes so great but Cinthias beames apeased?
What rage so feirce that love could not allay?

Twelve yeares intire I wasted in this warr,
Twelve yeares of my most happy younger dayes,
Butt I in them, and they now wasted ar,
Of all which past the sorrow only stayes.

So wrate I once, and my mishapp fortolde,
My minde still feelinge sorrowfull success
Yeven as before a storme the marbell colde
Douth by moyste teares tempestious tymes express.

So fealt my hevy minde my harmes att hande
Which my vayne thought in vayne sought to recure;
Att middell day my soonn seemde under land
When any littell cloude did it obscure.

And as the Isakells in a winters day
When as the soonn shines with unwounted warme,

So did my joyes mealt into secreat teares
So did my hart desolve in wastinge dropps;
And as the season of the year outweares
And heapes of snow from off the mountayn topps

With suddayne streames the vallies overflow,
So did the tyme draw on my more dispaire.
Then fludds of sorrow and whole seas of wo
The bancks of all my hope did overbeare

And dround my minde in deapts of missery.
Sumetyme I died, sumetyme I was distract,

My sowle the stage of fancies tragedye.
Then furious madness wher trew reason lackt

Wrate what it would, and scurgde myne own cansayte.
Oh, hevy hart who cann thee wittnes beare,
What tounge, what penn could thy tormentinge treat
But thyne owne mourning thoughts which present weare,

What stranger minde beleve the meanest part
What altered sence conceve the weakest wo
That tare, that rent, that peirsed thy sadd hart?

And as a man distract, with trebell might
Bound in stronge chaynes douth strive, and rage in vayne,
Till tyrde and breathless, he is forst to rest,
Fyndes by contention but increas of payne,
And fiery heat inflamde in swollen breast,

So did my minde in change of passion
From wo to wrath, from wrath returne to wo,
Struglinge in vayne from loves subjection.

Therefore all liveless, and all healpless bounde
My faytinge spirritts sunck, and hart apalde,
My joyes and hopes lay bleedinge on the ground
That not longe since the highest heaven scalde.

I hated life and cursed destiney
The thoughts of passed tymes like flames of hell,
Kyndled a fresh within my memorye
The many deere achievements that befell

In thos pryme yeares and infancy of love
Which to discribe weare butt to dy in writinge.
Ah those I sought, but vaynly, to remove
And vaynly shall, by which I perrish livinge.

And though strong reason holde before myne eyes
The Images, and formes of worlds past
Teachinge the cause why all thos flames that rize
From formes externall, cann no longer last,

Then that thos seeminge bewties hold in pryme
Loves ground, his essence, and his emperye,
All slaves to age, and vassalls unto tyme
Of which repentance writes the tragedye.

But this, my harts desire could not conceve
Whose Love outflew the fastest flyinge tyme;
A bewty that cann easely deseave
Th'arrest of yeares, and creepinge age outclyme,

A springe of bewties which tyme ripeth not
Tyme that butt workes onn frayle mortallety,
A sweetness which woes wronges outwipeth not,
Whom love hath chose for his devinnitye,

A vestall fier that burnes, but never wasteth,
That looseth nought by gevinge light to all
That endless shines eachwher and endless lasteth
Blossumes of pride than cann nor vade nor fall.

Thes weare thos marvelous perfections,
The parents of my sorrow and my envy
Most deathfull and most violent infections,
Thes be the Tirants that in fetters tye

Their wounded vassalls, yet nor kill nor cure,
But glory in their lastinge missery
That as her bewties would our woes should dure
Thes be the'effects of pourfull emperye.

Yet have thes wounders want which want cumpassion,
Yet hath her minde some markes of humayne race
Yet will shee bee a wooman for a fashion
So douth shee pleas her vertues to deface.

And like as that immortall pour douth seat
An element of waters to allay
The fiery soonn beames that on yearth do beate
And temper by cold night the heat of day,

So hath perfection, which begatt her minde,
Added therto a change of fantasye
And left her the affections of her kynde
Yet free from evry yevill but crueltye.

But leve her prayse, speak thow of nought but wo,
Write on the tale that Sorrow bydds thee tell,
Strive to forgett, and care no more to know
Thy cares are known, by knowinge thos too well,

Discribe her now as shee appeeres to thee,
Not as shee did apeere in dayes fordunn.
In love thos things that weare no more may bee,
For fancy seildume ends wher it begunn.

And as a streame by stronge hand bounded in
From natures course, wher it did sumetyme runn,
By some small rent or loose part douth beginn
To finde escape, till it a way hath woone,

Douth then all unawares in sunder teare
The forsed bounds and raginge, runn att large,
In th'auncient channells as they wounted weare,
Such is of weemens love the carefull charge,

Helde, and mayntaynde with multetude of woes,
Of longe arections such the suddayne fall.
Onn houre deverts, onn instant overthrowes
For which our lives, for which our fortunes thrale,

So many yeares thos joyes have deerely bought,
Of which when our fonde hopes do most assure
All is desolvde, our labors cume to nought,
Nor any marke therof ther douth indure;

No more then when small dropps of rayne do fall
Uppon the parched grounde by heat up dried,
No coolinge moysture is percevde att all
Nor any shew or signe of weet douth byde.

But as the feildes clothed with leves and floures
The bancks of roses smellinge pretious sweet
Have but ther bewties date, and tymely houres,
And then defast by winters cold, and sleet,

So farr as neather frute nor forme of floure
Stayes for a wittnes what such branches bare,
Butt as tyme gave, tyme did agayne devoure
And changde our risinge joy to fallinge care;

So of affection which our youth presented,
When shee that from the soonn reves poure and light
Did but decline her beames as discontented
Convertinge sweetest dayes to saddest night;

All droopes, all dyes, all troden under dust
The person, place, and passages forgotten
The hardest steele eaten with softest ruste,
The firme and sollide tree both rent and rotten;

Thos thoughts so full of pleasure and content
That in our absence weare affections foode
Ar rased out and from the fancy rent
In highest grace and harts deere care that stood,

Ar cast for pray to hatred, and to scorne,
Our deerest treasors and our harts trew joyes,
The tokens hunge onn brest, and kyndly worne
Ar now elcewhere disposde, or helde for toyes;

And thos which then our Jelosye removed,
And others for our sakes then valued deere,
The one forgot, the rest ar deere beloved,
When all of ours douth strange or wilde apeere.

Thos streames seeme standinge puddells which, before,
Wee saw our bewties in, so weare they cleere.
Bellphebes course is now observde no more,

That faire resemblance weareth out of date.
Our Ocean seas are but tempestius waves
And all things base that blessed wear of late . . .

And as a feilde wherin the stubbell stands
Of harvest past, the plowmans eye offends,
Hee tills agayne or teares them up with hands,
And throwes to fire as foylde and frutless ends,

And takes delight another seed to sow. . . .
So douth the minde root up all wounted thought
And scornes the care of our remayninge woes;
The sorrowes, which themsealvs for us have wrought,

Ar burnt to Cinders by new kyndled fiers,
The ashes ar dispeirst into the ayre,

The sythes, the grones of all our past desires
Ar cleane outworne, as things that never weare. . . .

With youth, is deade the hope of loves returne,
Who lookes not back to heare our after cryes.
Wher hee is not, hee laughts att thos that murne,
Whence hee is gonn, hee scornes the minde that dyes,

When hee is absent hee beleves no words,
When reason speakes hee careless stopps his ears,
Whom he hath left hee never grace affords
But bathes his wings in our lamentinge teares.

Unlastinge passion, soune outworne consayte
Whereon I built, and onn so dureless trust!
My minde had wounds, I dare not say desaite,
Weare I resolvde her promis was not Just.

Sorrow was my revendge, and wo my hate;
I pourless was to alter my desire.
My love is not of tyme, or bound to date
My harts internall heat, and livinge fier

Would not, or could be quencht, with suddayn shoures.
My bound respect was not confinde to dayes
My vowed fayth not sett to ended houres.
I love the bearinge and not bearinge sprayes

Which now to others do ther sweetness send,
Th'incarnat, snow driven white, and purest asure,
Who from high heaven douth on their feilds dissend
Fillinge their barns with grayne, and towres with treasure.

Erringe or never erringe, such is Love,
As while it lasteth scornes th'accompt of thos

Seekinge but sealf contentment to improve,
And hydes if any bee, his inward woes,

And will not know while hee knowes his own passion
The often and unjust perseverance
In deeds of love, and state, and every action
From that first day and yeare of their joyes entrance;

But I unblessed, and ill borne creature,
That did inebrace the dust, her boddy bearinge,
That loved her both, by fancy, and by nature,
That drew yeven with the milke in my first suckinge

Affection from the parents brest that bare mee,
Have found her as a stranger so severe
Improvinge my mishapp in each degree.
But love was gonn. So would I, my life weare!

A Queen shee was to mee, no more Belphebe,
A Lion then, no more a milke white Dove;
A prissoner in her brest I could not bee,
Shee did untye the gentell chaynes of love.

Love was no more the love of hydinge
All trespase, and mischance, for her own glorye.
It had bynn such, it was still for th'ellect,
But I must bee th'exampell in loves storye,
This was of all forpast the sadd effect. . . .

But thow my weery sowle and hevy thought
Made by her love a burden to my beinge,
Dust know my error never was forthought
Or ever could proceed from sence of Lovinge.

Of other cause if then it had proceedinge
I leve th'excuse syth Judgment hath bynn geven;
The lymes devided, sundred and a bleedinge
Cannot cumplayne the sentence was unyevunn.

This did that natures wonder, Vertues choyse,
The only parragonn of tymes begettinge
Devin in wordes, angellicall in voyse;
That springe of joyes, that floure of loves own settinge,

Th'Idea remayninge of thos golden ages,
That bewtye bravinge heavens, and yearth imbalminge,
Which after worthless worlds but play onn stages,
Such didsst thow her longe since discribe, yet sythinge,

That thy unabell spirrit could not fynde ought
In heavens bewties, or in yearths delighte
For likeness, fitt to satisfy thy thought.
Butt what hath it avaylde thee so to write?

Shee cares not for thy prayse, who knowes not thers;
Its now an Idell labor, and a tale
Tolde out of tyme that dulls the heerers eares;
A marchandise wherof ther is no sale.

Leve them, or lay them up with thy dispaires;
She hath resolvde, and Judged thee longe ago;
Thy lines ar now a murmeringe to her eares
Like to a fallinge streame which passinge sloe

Is wount to nurrishe sleap, and quietnes.
So shall thy paynfull labors bee perusde
And draw on rest, which sumetyme had regard.
But thos her cares, thy errors have excusde,

Thy dayes foredun have had ther dayes reward.
So her harde hart, so her estranged minde,
In which above the heavens, I once reposed,
So to thy error have her eares inclined,

And have forgotten all thy past deservinge,
Holdinge in minde butt only thyne offence
And only now affecteth thy depravinge
And thincks all vayne that pleadeth thy defence.

Yet greater fancye bewtye never bredd,
A more desire the hart bludd never nourished,
Her sweetness an affection never fedd
Which more in any age hath ever floryshedd.

The minde and vertue never have begotten
A firmer love, since love on yearth had poure,
A love obscurde, but cannot be forgotten,
Too great and stronge for tymes Jawes to devour;

Contayninge such a fayth as ages wound not,
Care, wackfull ever of her good estate,
Feare, dreadinge loss, which sythes, and joyes not
A memory, of the joyes her grace begate,

A lastinge gratfullness, for thos cumforts past
Of which the cordiall sweetness cannot dye.
Thes thoughts, knitt up by fayth, shall ever last,
Thes, tyme assayes, butt never can untye;

Whose life once lived in her perrellike brest,
Whose joyes weare drawne but from her happines,
Whose harts hygh pleasure, and whose minds trew rest
Proceeded from her fortunes blessedness,

Who was intentive, wakefull, and dismayde,
In feares, in dreames, in feeverus Jelosye,
Who longe in sylence served, and obayed
With secret hart, and hydden loyaltye;

Which never change to sadd adversetye,
Which never age, or natures overthrow,
Which never sickness, or deformetye,
Which never wastinge care, or weeringe wo,
If subject unto thes she could have bynn. . . .

Which never words, or witts mallicious,
Which never honors bayte, or worlds fame
Atchyved by attemptes adventerus,
Or ought beneath the soonn, or heavens frame,

Can so desolve, dissever, or distroye
The essentiall love, of no frayle parts cumpounded,
Though of the same now buried bee the joy,
The hope, the cumfort, and the sweetness ended,

But that the thoughts, and memories of thees
Worke a relapps of passion, and remayne
Of my sadd harte the sorrow suckinge bees.
The wrongs recevde, the scornes perswade in vayne. . . .

And though thes medcines worke desire to end
And ar in others the trew cure of likinge,
The salves that heale loves wounds and do amend
Consuminge woe, and slake our harty sythinge,

They worke not so, in thy minds long deseas:
Externall fancy tyme alone recurethe
All whose effects do weare away with ease.
Love of delight while such delight indureth
Stayes by the pleasure, but no longer stayes. . . .

But in my minde so is her love inclosde
And is therof not only the best parte
But into it the essence is disposde. . . .
Oh love (the more my wo) to it thow art

Yeven as the moysture in each plant that growes,
Yeven as the soonn unto the frosen ground,
Yeven as the sweetness, to th'incarnate rose,
Yeven as the Center in each perfait rounde,

As water to the fyshe, to men as ayre,
As heat to fier, as light unto the soonn.
Oh love it is but vayne, to say thow weare,
Ages, and tymes, cannot thy poure outrun. . . .

Thow are the sowle of that unhappy minde
Which beinge by nature made an Idell thought
Begon yeven then to take immortall kynde
When first her vertues in thy spirrights wrought. . . .

From thee therfore that mover cannot move
Because it is becume thy cause of beinge;
What ever error may obscure that love
What ever frayle effect of mortall livinge,

What ever passion from distempered hart
What absence, tyme, or injuries effect,
What faythless frinds, or deipe dissembled art
Present, to feede her most unkynde suspect.

Yet as the eayre in deip caves under ground
Is strongly drawne when violent heat hath rent
Great clefts therin, till moysture do abound,
And then the same imprisoned, and uppent,

Breakes out in yearthquakes teringe all asunder,
So in the Center of my cloven hart,
My hart, to whom her bewties wear such wounder,
Lyes the sharpe poysoned heade of that loves dart,

Which till all breake and all desolve to dust
Thence drawne it cannot bee, or therin knowne.
Ther, mixt with my hart bludd, the fretting rust
The better part hath eaten, and outgrown. . . .

Butt what of thos, or thes, or what of ought
Of that which was, or that which is, to treat?
What I possess is butt the same I sought;
My love was falce, my labors weare desayte.

Nor less then such they ar esteemde to bee,
A fraude bought att the prize of many woes,
A guile, whereof the profitts unto mee—
Coulde it be thought premeditate for thos?

Wittnes thos withered leves left on the tree,
The sorrow worren face, the pensive minde,
The externall shews what may th'internall bee;
Cold care hath bitten both the root, and rind, . . .

Butt stay my thoughts, make end, geve fortune way,
Harshe is the voice of woe and sorrows sounde,
Cumplaynts cure not, and teares do but allay
Greifs for a tyme, which after more abounde.

To seeke for moysture in th'Arabien sande
Is butt a losse of labor, and of rest.
The lincks which tyme did break of harty bands

Words cannot knytt, or waylings make a new.
Seeke not the soonn in cloudes, when it is sett. . . .

On highest mountaynes wher thos Sedars grew,
Agaynst whose bancks, the trobled ocean bett,

And weare the markes to finde thy hoped port,
Into a soyle farr off them sealves remove,
On Sestus shore, Leanders late resorte,
Hero hath left no lampe to Guyde her love;

Thow lookest for light in vayne, and stormes arise;
Shee sleaps thy death that erst thy danger syth-ed
Strive then no more, bow down thy weery eyes,
Eyes, which to all thes woes thy hart have guided.

Shee is gonn, Shee is lost! Shee is found, shee is ever faire!
Sorrow drawes weakly, wher love drawes not too.
Woes cries, sound nothinge, butt only in loves eare.
Do then by Dyinge, what life cannot doo. . . .

Unfolde thy flockes, and leve them to the feilds
To feed on hylls, or dales, wher likes them best,
Of what the summer, or the springe tyme yeildes,
For love, and tyme, hath geven thee leve to rest.

Thy hart, which was their folde, now in decay
By often stormes, and winters many blasts
All torne and rent, becumes misfortunes pray,
Falce hope, my shepherds staff, now age hath brast.

My pipe, which loves own hand, gave my desire
To singe her prayses, and my wo uppon,
Dispaire hath often threatned to the fier,
As vayne to keipe now all the rest ar gonn.

Thus home I draw, as deaths longe night drawes onn.
Yet every foot, olde thoughts turne back myne eyes,

Constraynt mee guides as old age drawes a stonn
Agaynst the hill, which over wayghty lyes

For feebell armes, or wasted strength to move.
My steapps are backwarde, gasinge on my loss,
My minds affection, and my sowles sole love,
Not mixte with fancies chafe, or fortunes dross.

To God I leve it, who first gave it me,
And I her gave, and she returnd agayne,
As it was herrs. So lett his mercies bee,
Of my last cumforts, the essentiall meane.
    But be it so, or not, th'effects, are past.
    Her love hath end; my woe must ever last.

*The end of the bookes, of the Oceans love to Scinthia,
and the beginninge of the 12 Boock, entreatinge of
Sorrow*

My dayes delights, my springetyme joies fordunn,
Which in the dawne, and risinge soonn of youth
Had their creation, and weare first begunn,

Do in the yeveninge, and the winter sadd,
Present my minde, which takes my tymes accompt,
The greif remayninge of the joy it had.

My tymes that then rann ore them sealves in thes,
And now runn out in others happines,
Bring unto thos new joyes, and new borne dayes.

So could shee not, if shee weare not the soonn,
Which sees the birth, and buriall, of all elce,
And holds that poure, with which shee first begunn;

Levinge each withered boddy to be torne
By fortune, and by tymes tempestius,
Which by her vertu, once faire frute have borne,

Knowinge shee cann renew, and cann create
Green from the grounde, and floures, yeven out of stone,
By vertu lastinge over tyme and date,

Levinge us only woe, which like the moss,
Havinge cumpassion of unburied bones
Cleaves to mischance, and unrepayred loss.

For tender stalkes——

The Lie

Goe soule the bodies guest
     upon a thankelesse arrant,
Feare not to touch the best
     the truth shall be thy warrant:
Goe since I needs must die,
     and give the world the lie.

Say to the Court it glowes,
     and shines like rotten wood,
Say to the Church it showes
     what's good, and doth no good.
If Church and Court reply,
     then give them both the lie.

Tell Potentates they live
   acting by others action,
Not loved unlesse they give,
   not strong but by affection.
If Potentates reply,
   give Potentates the lie.

Tell men of high condition,
   that mannage the estate,
Their purpose is ambition,
   their practise onely hate:
And if they once reply,
   then give them all the lie.

Tell them that brave it most,
   they beg for more by spending,
Who in their greatest cost
   seek nothing but commending.
And if they make replie,
   then give them all the lie.

Tell zeale it wants devotion
   tell love it is but lust
Tell time it meets but motion,
   tell flesh it is but dust.
And wish them not replie
   for thou must give the lie.

Tell age it daily wasteth,
   tell honour how it alters.
Tell beauty how she blasteth
   tell favour how it falters
And as they shall reply,
   give every one the lie.

Tell wit how much it wrangles
   in tickle points of nycenesse,
Tell wisedome she entangles
   her selfe in over wisenesse.
And when they doe reply
   straight give them both the lie.

Tell Phisicke of her boldnes,
   tell skill it is prevention:
Tell charity of coldnes,
   tell law it is contention,
And as they doe reply
   so give them still the lie.

Tell fortune of her blindnesse,
   tell nature of decay,
Tell friendship of unkindnesse,
   tell justice of delay.
And if they will reply,
   then give them all the lie.

Tell Arts they have no soundnesse,
   but vary by esteeming,
Tell schooles they want profoundnes
   and stand too much on seeming.
If Art and schooles reply,
   give arts and schooles the lie.

Tell faith its fled the Citie,
   tell how the country erreth,
Tell manhood shakes off pittie,
   tell vertue least preferreth
And if they doe reply,
   spare not to give the lie.

So when thou hast as I,
    commanded thee, done blabbing,
Although to give the lie,
    deserves no lesse then stabbing,
Stab at thee he that will,
    no stab thy soule can kill.

Sir Walter Rawleigh to his sonne

Three thinges there bee that prosper up apace
And flourish, whilest they growe a sunder farr,
But on a day, they meet all in one place,
And when they meet, they one an other marr;
And they bee theise, the wood, the weede, the wagg.
The wood is that, which makes the Gallow tree,
The weed is that, which stringes the Hangmans bagg,
The wagg my pritty knave betokeneth thee.
Marke well deare boy whilest theise assemble not,
Green springs the tree, hempe growes, the wagg is wilde,
But when they meet, it makes the timber rott,
It frets the halter, and it choakes the childe.
    Then bless thee, and beware, and lett us praye,
    Wee part not with thee at this meeting day.

The passionate mans Pilgrimage
Supposed to be Written by One at the Point of Death

Give me my Scallop shell of quiet,
My staffe of Faith to walke upon
My Scrip of Joy, Immortall diet,

63

My bottle of salvation:
My Gowne of Glory, hopes true gage,
And thus Ile take my pilgrimage.

Blood must be my bodies balmer,
No other balme will there be given
Whilst my soule like a white Palmer
Travels to the land of heaven,
Over the silver mountaines,
Where spring the Nectar fountaines:
And there Ile kisse
The Bowle of blisse,
And drink my eternall fill
On every milken hill.
My soule will be a drie before,
But after it, will nere thirst more.

And by the happie blisfull way
More peacefull Pilgrims I shall see,
That have shooke off their gownes of clay,
And goe appareld fresh like mee.
Ile bring them first
To slake their thirst,
And then to tast those Nectar suckets
At the cleare wells
Where sweetnes dwells,
Drawne up by Saints in Christall buckets.

And when our bottles and all we,
Are fild with immortalitie:
Then the holy paths weele travell
Strewde with Rubies thicke as gravell,
Seelings of Diamonds, Saphire floores,
High walles of Corall and Pearle Bowres.

From thence to heavens Bribeles hall
Where no corrupted voyces brall,
No Conscience molten into gold,
Nor forg'd accusers bought and sold,
No cause deferd, nor vaine spent Jorney,
For there Christ is the Kings Atturney:
Who pleades for all without degrees,
And he hath Angells, but no fees.

When the grand twelve million Jury,
Of our sinnes and sinfull fury,
Gainst our soules blacke verdicts give,
Christ pleades his death, and then we live,
Be thou my speaker taintles pleader,
Unblotted Lawer, true proceeder,
Thou movest salvation even for almes:
Not with a bribed Lawyers palmes.

And this is my eternall plea,
To him that made Heaven, Earth and Sea,
Seeing my flesh must die so soone,
And want a head to dine next noone,
Just at the stroke when my vaines start and spred
Set on my soule an everlasting head.
Then am I readie like a palmer fit,
To tread those blest paths which before I writ.

On the Life of Man

What is our life? a play of passion,
Our mirth the musicke of division,
Our mothers wombes the tyring houses be,
Where we are drest for this short Comedy,

Heaven the Judicious sharpe spectator is,
That sits and markes still who doth act amisse,
Our graves that hide us from the searching Sun,
Are like drawne curtaynes when the play is done,
Thus march we playing to our latest rest,
Onely we dye in earnest, that's no Jest.

To the Translator of Lucan

Had *Lucan* hid the truth to please the time,
He had beene too unworthy of thy Penne:
Who never sought, nor ever car'd to clime
By flattery, or seeking worthlesse men.
For this thou hast been bruis'd: but yet those scarres
Do beautifie no lesse, then those wounds do
Receiv'd in just, and in religious warres;
Though thou hast bled by both, and bearst them too.
Change not, to change thy fortune tis too late.
Who with a manly faith resolves to dye,
May promise to himselfe a lasting state,
Though not so great, yet free from infamy.
    Such was thy *Lucan*, whom so to translate
    Nature thy Muse (like LUCANS) did create.

Metrical Translations from The History of the World

The Sunne may set and rise:
But we contrariwise
Sleepe after our short light
One everlasting night.

                        (Catullus, Carm., v. 4–6)

The Aegyptians thinke it sinne to roote up, or to bite
Their Leekes or Onyons, which they serve with holy rite:
O happie Nations, which of their owne sowing
Have store of Gods in every garden growing.

(Juvenal, xv. 9–11)

If all this world had no originall,
But things have ever beene as now they are:
Before the siege of Thebes or Troyes last fall,
   Why did no Poet sing some elder warre?

(Lucretius, v. 325–8)

Many by valour have deserv'd renowne
   Ere Agamemnon: yet lye all opprest
Under long night unwept for and unknowne:
   For with no sacred Poet were they blest.

(Horace, Od. IV. ix. 25–8)

I am that Dido which thou here do'st see,
Cunningly framed in beauteous Imagrie.
Like this I was, but had not such a soule,
As Maro fained, incestuous and foule.
Aeneas never with his Trojan host
Beheld my face, or landed on this coast.
But flying proud Iarbas villanie,
Not mov'd by furious love or jealousie;
I did with weapon chast, to save my fame,
Make way for death untimely, ere it came.
This was my end; but first I built a Towne,
Reveng'd my husbands death, liv'd with renowne.
Why did'st thou stirre up Virgil, envious Muse,
Falsely my name and honour to abuse?
Readers, beleeve Historians; not those

Which to the world Joves thefts and vice expose.
Poets are liers, and for verses sake
Will make the Gods of humane crimes partake.

(Ausonius, Epigr. cxviii)

Conjectural First Draft of the Petition to Queen Anne

My dayes delight, my spring tyme joyes foredun,
Which in the dawne and rysing Sunne of youth
Had their creation and were first begun,

Doe in the Evening, and the Winter sad,
Present my Mynde (which takes my times account)
The griefe remayning of the joye it had.

For as noe fortune stands, soe noe Mans Love
Stayes by the wretched and disconsolate,
All old affections from new sorrowes Move.

Mosse to unburied bones, Ivie to walles,
Whom Life and people have abandond,
Till th'one be rotten, stayes, till th'other falles;

But friendships, kindred, and Loves Memorie
Dies sole, extinguisht hearing or behoulding
The voyce of woe, or face of Miserie;

Who being in all like those Winter showers
Doe come uncald, but then forebear to fall
When parching heate hath burnt both leaves and flowers;

And what we some tyme were we seeme noe More,
Fortune hath changd our shapes, and Destinie
Defac'd our very forme we had before.

For did in Cinders any heate remayne
Of those cleare fyres of Love and friendlines
I could not call for right and call in vaine.

Or had Truth power the guiltles could not fall
Malice, vaine-glorie, and revenge tryumph;
But Truth alone cannot encounter all.

All Love, and all desert of former tymes
Malice hath covered from my Soveraignes Eyes
And Largely laide abroade supposed Crymes,

Burying the former with their Memorie,
Teaching offence to speake before it goe,
Disguising private hate with publique dutie.

But Mercie is fled to God that Mercie Made,
Compassion dead, fayth turn'd to policie,
Which knowes not those which sit in sorrowes shade.

Cold walles to you I speake, but you are senclesse;
Celestiall poweres, you heard, but have determined
And shall determyne to the greatest happinesse.

To whom then shall I Crie, to whom shall wronge
Cast downe her teares, or hould up foulded handes?
To her to whom remorse doth most belonge,

To her that is the first and may alone
Be called Impresse of the Brittaines.
Who should have Mercie if a Queen have none?

Who should resist stronge hate, fierce Injurie,
Or who releive th'oppressed state of Truth,
Who is Companion els to powerfull Majestie

But you, great, godliest, powerfull princesse,
Who have brought glorie and posteritie
Unto this widdowe Land and people hopelesse?

Sir W. Raleigh, On the Snuff of a Candle the night before he died

Cowards fear to Die, but Courage stout,
Rather than Live in Snuff, will be put out.

These verses following were made by Sir Walter Rawleigh the night before he died and left att the Gate howse

Even such is tyme which takes in trust
Our yowth, our Joyes, and all we have,
And payes us butt with age and dust:
Who in the darke and silent grave
When we have wandred all our wayes
Shutts up the storye of our dayes.
And from which earth and grave and dust
The Lord shall rayse me up I trust.

Index of First Lines